Kid

What's So Great About Queen Elizabeth I?

A Biography of Queen Elizabeth Just for Kids!

Sam Rogers

KidLit-O Books

www.kidlito.com

Table of Contents

About KidCaps

KidLit-O is an imprint of BookCaps™ that is just for kids! Each month BookCaps will be releasing several books in this exciting imprint. Visit are website or like us on Facebook to see more!

To add your name to our mailing list, visit this link: **http://www.kidlito.com/mailing-list.html**

Introduction

The young woman walked thoughtfully through the garden, dragging her feet through the leaves that had fallen and collected on the ground around her. The gardeners had yet to collect them, and she took advantage of that fact to crunch leaves as many as she could with each step, bringing a slight smile to her otherwise worried face. This young woman had a lot on her mind today, and even though she was walking the grounds of a beautiful house and all her needs were taken care of, her eyebrows showed that she was deep in thought and concerned about something.

At just 25 years old, Elizabeth, daughter of Henry VIII, had known her share of troubles and sorrow. Disowned by her father the King while just a child, accused by her sister of a crime she did not commit, and sentenced to serve life in prison by the Queen of England, Elizabeth found herself in a sort of exile. She was forced to leave the only city she had ever known and the people she loved to live out the rest of her life under house arrest – far away from anyone who knew her or loved her.

Perhaps a weaker person would have cried and would have given up on life. Maybe a different girl would have felt sorry for herself and forgotten about the world she left behind. But Elizabeth didn't do any of those things - that simply was not her way of handling challenges or setbacks.

For one year, Elizabeth, the daughter of King Henry VIII, had walked in this garden, much as she was doing today. And during each walk, she thought long and hard about the important family that she had been born into, and about the life that rightfully should be hers. For too long, her relatives in the Royal House of Tudor had fought over who would sit down on the throne of England and had worried more about their own concerns and not about the lives of their subjects. And for too long, nations like Spain had made England look foolish on the world scene.

In the years before she became Queen, England had suffered one scandal after another, including assassination plots and religious persecution. All of this civil unrest had led to fighting in the streets. English citizens were killing each other over their personal beliefs, and each side refused to listen to what the other had to say. Someone needed to step up and unite the country, and Queen Elizabeth wanted to be that person.

She wanted to fix England's problems, both at home and abroad. But how could she possibly do that while a prisoner far away from the capital city of London?

On this cold November morning in the year 1558, Elizabeth knew that her life might finally change. She had heard reports that the current Queen (her half-sister) was very ill and the throne would soon be vacant. Elizabeth had even made preparations just in case she inherited the throne. She talked to important people, got the support of a team, and shared her revolutionary ideas with them just in case she ever got out of this place.

Sitting beneath a tall tree, Elizabeth looked small by comparison. She did not have the strength of the guards who kept her prisoner in this house, and she could never hope to overpower them by fighting. But what Elizabeth lacked in physical strength she made up for in intelligence: Elizabeth knew how to rule a country.

As she sat beneath the tree, a messenger came bursting out of the house and went directly towards her, kicking up the fallen leaves in his desperate run. Her thoughts interrupted,

Elizabeth's heart began to beat as he drew near. The moment he arrived, the messenger spoke the words that changed Elizabeth's life forever: "Her Majesty Queen Mary died this morning."

Lifting her chin, Elizabeth quoted a particularly appropriate section from the Bible's Book of Psalms: "It is the Lord's doing, and it is marvelous in our eyes."

Standing up, Elizabeth turned to her servant and told her to get some things ready. Elizabeth would be leaving this place soon to secure her place on throne as Queen of England. Once she sat on the throne, she knew exactly what she would do: she would have to put an end to the religious fighting: get the support of the people, and let the world know that England was a powerful nation and was not to be trifled with. She would make sure that England became a true Empire that would live on long after she had died.

And against all odds, this 25 year old young woman would eventually accomplish all she set out to do.

Elizabeth reigned as Queen of England as the last representative of the Tudor Dynasty, which was started by her grandfather, King Henry VII. Beginning in 1558 when she was just 25 years old, Elizabeth ruled as Queen for some 44 years until her death in 1603. She used her natural intelligence and all the education and training that she had received to help those around her. She never married (leading to her nickname "the Virgin Queen"), feeling that her time and energy would be better spent caring for the needs of her country.

In a time when many kings and queens took advantage of those below them, Elizabeth tried to really understand how her citizens felt about life, what their concerns were, and how she could use her position to help them. She gave beautiful speeches, kings and princes proposed marriage to her, and she worked hard to increase the standard of living for the people of England that she loved so much.

The decisions Elizabeth made during her time on the throne brought much prosperity and happiness to the people of England, so much so that the entire time period is now known as "Elizabethan England." Artists like Shakespeare thrived during her reign, and other nations were forced to acknowledge that England was indeed a country that needed to be respected.

As a result of her efforts to bring everyone in England closer together, Elizabeth came to be called "Good Queen Bess" and "Gloriana" (a name taken from a poem written about her) by her citizens. Hundreds of years later, the people of England still look to this marvelous woman and are thankful for all of her hard work.

But things didn't start out so well for this amazing and dynamic young woman. Disowned by her father, chased out of the royal palace by her stepmother, and imprisoned in the Tower of London after being falsely accused of trying to kill the Queen, Elizabeth had fought her share of personal battles during her life.

She was born on September 7, 1553 to King Henry VIII and his second wife, Anne Boleyn. Life may have started out pleasantly enough, living in the royal palace with her father the King – but things wouldn't stay so pleasant for long.

Chapter 1: The Early Life and Education of Queen Elizabeth I

Elizabeth's father (King Henry VIII) was married a total of six times. Five of his marriages ended early (either in death or annulment), and his last wife survived him after his death. With three of his wives Henry fathered three children: Mary, Elizabeth, and Edward.

2   Image   source: https://encrypted-tbn1.gstatic.com/images?q=tbn:ANd9GcR0_rQ1K8fSgZABdVdN

Unlike many stable homes around the world, at times the royal house of England seemed more like a play than a model family. The many wives of Henry VIII came and went in a strange sort of parade, and as each one left, people whispered about why the marriage had ended. On occasion, there were lies and false accusations that led to the wife being executed, and before long, a pretty new face would appear at the King's side. Despite the strange goings on, the citizens and members of the court were supposed to act like everything was business as usual.

Here is a brief overview of the six marriages of Henry VIII:

- he annulled his marriage to first wife (Catherine of Aragon, the mother of Mary);
- he beheaded his second wife (Anne Boleyn, the mother of Elizabeth);
- his third wife (Jane Seymour) died shortly after giving birth to his son (Edward);
- he annulled his marriages to his fourth and fifth wives (Anne of Cleves and Catherine Howard);

- he died while married to his sixth wife (Catherine Parr).

Some people use this rhyme to help them remember:

King Henry the Eighth,
to six wives he was wedded.
One died, one survived,
two annulled, two beheaded.

Although he didn't fight many wars, King Henry VIII was a good king in that he tried to make sure that the country would have plenty of money after he was gone. He wanted his son (who became King Edward VI) to help make England as strong as possible. He knew that a large amount of money could do a lot for making a king more effective.

But for his entire life before the birth of Edward, King Henry had been obsessed with fathering a son who would take over after he died. He had two daughters (one with Catherine of Aragon and one with Anne Boleyn), but he couldn't stand the idea of one of his daughters (Mary or Elizabeth) running things after he was gone.

While it may seem like a small thing, in some ways this obsession with having a male heir who would inherit the throne caused a lot of problems for both his family, and for the entire country. Henry caused more harm and took away his nation's peace for years because of his unreasonable idea.

Apparently not understanding the basics of biology (which say that the father – not the mother – is the one who determines the sex of the child), Henry blamed his wives for not giving him the son he wanted so much. Henry VIII went to great lengths to get a son. In his obsession, he would annul marriages and cause a religious revolution in his country – one that would eventually lead to many deaths and civil unrest. How?

Henry's desire to marry one wife after anther was in direct conflict with the teachings of the Catholic Church. England was a Catholic country, which meant that the King was supposed to obey the laws of the Pope.

King Henry VIII was a powerful and persuasive man, and after Catherine of Aragon failed to give birth to a son, he got special permission from the local representative of the Pope (the Archbishop of Canterbury) to annul his marriage with Catherine of Aragon. But by ignoring what the Pope said about marriage and doing what he thought was best, King Henry

VIII set into motion a series of events that would lead to years of unrest and hundreds of deaths.

Annulling his marriage to Catherine of Aragon pulled England away from the Catholic Church and later brought it under the authority of the newly-created Church of England, and not everyone was happy with this change. As King Henry went from one wife to another, many English citizens protested the religious changes he had made and said that they wanted to go back to being Catholics. In fact, this fight over religions and which Church to belong to would become a big problem later on after King Henry died.

It was during this time of trouble that Elizabeth was born. Her father was not happy to see that, instead of having a son, he now had two daughters. So, as he had already done with Catherine of Aragon, he blamed Elizabeth's mother Anne Boleyn for not giving him a boy. It wasn't long before Henry annulled his marriage with Anne. But things didn't stop there.

When Elizabeth was just 2 years old her mother was arrested, taken to the Tower of London, and beheaded after being accused of various crimes: being unfaithful to her husband, committing treason, and being a witch.

By the time Anne Boleyn was executed, Henry had already started to date his next wife, making some historians think that Henry may have lied when accusing Anne. He may have wanted to get her out of the way so that he could hurry up and get married to this new woman.

When Henry VIII annulled his marriage to Elizabeth's mother, he also disowned Elizabeth. In other words, he pretended like Elizabeth wasn't his daughter, and that he would never leave anything to her. Even though the King took some steps to make sure that she had everything she needed and that she received a good education, this decision meant that Elizabeth would not be recognized as the daughter of the King or as a member of the royal family. Most important of all, it meant she wasn't in line to inherit the throne when Henry VIII died.

It's not hard to imagine how Elizabeth felt as she grew up: her mother was dead, her half-sister was far away in another town with another family, and her father wanted nothing to do with her. Things got even worse once Henry's third wife (Jane Seymour) gave birth to a son who they named Edward. Now that Henry finally had the son that he had been waiting for his whole life, there was no doubt that the King had no room in his heart for Elizabeth.

In many ways, Elizabeth had been completely forgotten by the royal house of England.

And things may have stayed that way forever if Henry's sixth and last wife (Catherine Parr) wouldn't have convinced the King to once again include his daughters in the royal line of succession. Catherine had special affection for Elizabeth and loved to spend time with her, going so far as to adopt the young girl and to let her live in her house. Catherine made sure that Elizabeth continued to receive good care and a first rate education.

Some years later, in 1547, Elizabeth's father King Henry VIII died.

Elizabeth was about 14 years old, and it is possible that she felt some sadness when she heard the news. Even though she hadn't really known her mother and her father did not treat her with much affection, what teenage girl doesn't want the guidance and support of her parents? Even though she, Lady Elizabeth, at times still felt like an orphan, alone in the world now that both of her parents were gone.

Her half-brother Edward VI became King at just 9 years old, and Catherine Parr remarried (a man named Thomas Seymour) as Elizabeth tried to find some sort of stability in her life.

But it wasn't long before scandal yet again plagued Elizabeth and the Tudor dynasty.

Catherine Parr felt that Elizabeth and her new husband Thomas were growing too close, and Catherine even suspected that the two were developing romantic feelings for each other (which would be very inappropriate as Thomas was a grown man and Elizabeth was still a girl). Not sure of the best way to handle the situation, Catherine didn't say anything for some time. But after one particularly ugly episode where Catherine is said to have caught the two hugging each other, Lady Elizabeth was sent away from the Parr house and never saw her stepmother again. Within a year or so, Catherine would be dead from childbirth, and Elizabeth would lose her last contact in the royal house.

Edward became King when he was just 9 years old, but only reigned for six years before dying of illness. To honor his father's wishes, Edward did all that was in his power to make sure the country stayed separate from the Catholic Church, too. He went so far as to change his will so that Mary (who was a very strong Catholic) could not inherit the throne. But because he couldn't cut out one sister and leave the other,

Elizabeth – who actually supported the Church of England – was also removed from the line of succession.

This change was illegal, but the people around the King did not try to stop him. Perhaps they also were worried about what might happen with a Catholic Queen in power. Young Edward knew that he was dying, and so he wrote in his

3   Image   source: http://upload.wikimedia.org/wikipedia/commons/4/4f/Edward_VI_of_England_c._1546.jpg

will that it would be his cousin Lady Jane Grey (who was loyal to the Church of England) who would sit on the throne when he died.

And in 1553 that is exactly what happened. Edward's sickness took his life, and his cousin Jane Grey sat down on the throne as Queen of England...for less than two weeks.

Because the will that gave Jane the throne was made illegally in the first place, Edward and Elizabeth's sister Mary fought against it, and got a lot of supporters to march on the capital with her. So less than two weeks after becoming queen, Lady Jane Grey was forced to leave the throne and to give it to Mary. One of Mary's first acts as Queen was to imprison the former Queen of England, who years later would be executed along with her husband on an unrelated charge of treason.

Elizabeth was about 20 years old when all this happened.

By that time, Elizabeth had gone through a lot of harrowing experiences in her life: she had lost her father, mother, and half-brother in death; she had been exiled twice from the royal house - once after being disowned and once after being accused of improper behavior – and she had seen four different people sit on the throne of England in a span of less than seven years.

All around her, people were fighting over which member of the Tudor dynasty should be in charge and what kinds of decisions would be best for the country. In a time of so much chaos, it is not hard to understand why Elizabeth felt sad for her country. She saw suffering each day and all she wanted was to be able to help the people around her – but her half-sister Mary would never let Elizabeth anywhere near a position of power. In fact, it wasn't long before Mary started to think of Elizabeth – her own half-sister – as an enemy.

Mary was a strong supporter of the Catholic Church and did everything in her power to make it the only religion in the country. Her extreme attitude made her think that it was alright to kill anyone who didn't agree that her religion was the only way to worship God. Historians say that Queen Mary executed at least 280 people during her five year reign. Those executions were not of treasonous soldiers or spies; they had been people who simply didn't agree with the Queen's religious opinions. As a result, people began to call Elizabeth's sister "Bloody Mary".

Shortly after becoming Queen, some citizens organized a plot against Mary, and one of the conspirators was Sir Thomas Wyatt, a friend of Elizabeth. Even though there was no direct evidence against Elizabeth, the Queen was convinced that she had been involved in the plan. Mary refused to listen to anything that Elizabeth or anyone else had to say in her defense, and the judgment was swift.

Under the cover of darkness one night, the Queen had Elizabeth arrested and sent to the infamous Tower of London, the same place where Elizabeth's mother was imprisoned and executed. Once a fort, this fortified stone building on the bank of the River Thames became a jail reserved for the upper part of society. While it was not as dirty and disease-filled as a common jailhouse, the Tower of London was still a prison and people were still executed there.

Elizabeth was brought in at night through a special gate reserved for the worst criminals: traitors against the country. She at first refused to go into the prison, perhaps thinking of her mother and the fate that she had suffered. But eventually she was taken to a cell, and she spent the next two months of her life in that small room waiting to see what would happen to her. Would she spend the rest of her life in the Tower of London? Would she be exiled from the country? Would she be burned at the stake like other so-called "traitors" had been?

As it turned out, Mary decided not to execute her sister, and allowed Elizabeth a certain amount of freedom. But instead of letting her stay in London, where other might see her and decide to form another conspiracy, Mary sent Elizabeth far away where she wouldn't be a threat.

Elizabeth was sent to the town of Woodstock where she lived under house arrest, and was watched over by a guard.

5

When the time came for her to be moved from the Tower of London to her new home in Woodstock, crowds of people lined the streets on the way to cheer for and show their support for this mistreated Lady and daughter of the King.

5   Image   source: http://upload.wikimedia.org/wikipedia/commons/7/74/Hatfield_Ho use_Old_Palace.jpg

As Queen, Mary kept her distance from her younger half-sister Elizabeth (with the exception of one visit Elizabeth made to Mary when it looked like the Queen might be pregnant and giving birth). But when Mary failed to have a child and it became clear that her swollen belly was a symptom of an illness, everyone realized that when she died there would be no one to take her place on the throne. There was only one person who could lead the country after Mary died.

Elizabeth would be the next Queen of England.

For three more years, Elizabeth was kept prisoner at Hatfield House in Woodstock, but she used her time well. She made plans and contacts and shared her ideas with others. Instead of depending on her own intelligence, Elizabeth decided she would surround herself with the smartest people she could find and would listen to what they had to say before making important decisions.

There was a little more intrigue as Mary got sicker and sicker: Mary's husband (King Philip II of Spain) began to think of ways to keep his presence in England. He knew that once Mary died he wouldn't have any connections in the royal court, so he did the unthinkable: before his wife had even died he tried to see if Elizabeth would marry him! Of course, Elizabeth did not accept this strange proposal from her sister's husband, and so when Queen Mary died on November 17, 1558, Elizabeth alone inherited the throne and became Queen of England.

In just one moment, Elizabeth had gone from being a prisoner in Woodstock to being the most powerful person in the whole country!

The arrangements that Elizabeth had made while under house arrest proved very useful and she was able to begin her work as Queen without wasting any time. She had her first Council of State (meeting with important officials) while still at the house in Woodstock, and took definite steps to fix the problems of England.

It had been a long and troublesome road, but Elizabeth was finally about to sit down on the throne and take her rightful place as Queen. But how could she unite a nation that had been bitterly divided for years? And how could she make sure that the average English subject's concerns were addressed?

Chapter 2: The Career of Queen Elizabeth I

Because she had been abused by the Kings and Queens of England for so many years, Lady Elizabeth had sworn that she would act differently if she ever got to be the one in charge. No matter how much authority she got and not matter how many people supported her, she would never let her own opinions be so strong that they ruined the lives of others, and she would never forget about the men and women who relied on her for protection and help.

Shortly after becoming Queen, Elizabeth took steps to bring the people of her country together, starting with the divisive issue of religion.

Elizabeth knew that there were very strong opinions on both sides of the issue: the Catholic Church on one side said that the people should only listen to the King or Queen if the Pope recognized her, and if she swore to obey everything the Pope said. On the other side, the Church of England (founded by Elizabeth's father King Henry VIII) said that the Pope wasn't the boss of England and that the King (or

Queen) is the one who should be the religious leader for the people.

Sometimes it seemed like the two sides would never find anything to agree on. Too many nasty things had been said, and too many people had been killed.

But whatever her personal beliefs and feelings might have been, Elizabeth put them to one side so that she could find a peaceful solution. She refused to sit in judgment of others, once saying that it wasn't her place to "make windows into men's souls ... there is only one Jesus Christ and all the rest is a dispute over trifles".[6]

Elizabeth's attitude - of not rushing to judgment or forcing her religious beliefs on anyone - was completely different from what other members of her family had done: her father had created a new religion to justify his desire to get married more than once; her brother illegally changed his will to make sure the next ruler would obey his father's religion; and her sister murdered anyone who held different religious opinions than she did.

---

[6] Quotation source: https://www.royal.gov.uk/HistoryoftheMonarchy/KingsandQueens ofEngland/TheTudors/ElizabethI.aspx

Instead of following those bad examples, Elizabeth decided to let the good of the majority outweigh the opinions of the few. So instead of trying to please the fanatical religious people on either side who were willing to kill their countrymen over personal beliefs, Elizabeth worked to find a way to make everyone happy. After talking with her counselors, she found the perfect solution: she would keep the best of both religions.

There was no way to simply avoid the religion issue; she had to take a side. But she would do so in a way that would be less likely to anger the people around her. In 1559, in a move known as the Elizabethan Religious Settlement, Elizabeth passed laws that kept the Church of England as the official religion but which made sure that it would include lots of symbols, ideas, and customs from the Catholic Church. That way, both groups had something to be happy about.

Although there was some difficulty in getting Catholic politicians to support this new law (and the Pope himself later kicked Elizabeth out of the Catholic Church, and threatened to do the same to anyone who supported her), eventually most people accepted the new religious arrangement and enjoyed real peace for the first time in years. Instead of killing each other in the streets and being afraid of a Queen who killed them for their beliefs, the people could finally work for the good of the nation.

It's true that the Pope's decision to kick Elizabeth out of his Church resulted in some trouble for her and in some plots against her life, but the troubles were nothing that she and her private security network couldn't handle.

While still a prisoner, Elizabeth had assembled a special team of very smart people (called a Privy Council), and her right-hand man and leader of that team was named William Cecil. Cecil handled the kingdom's money and, together with Francis Walsingham, established a network of spies working for the throne. Together, Cecil, Walsingham, and the spies (called the Secret Service) warned Elizabeth of dangers against her life and position as Queen. This team would be with Elizabeth for much of her 44 year reign and would guide her through many difficult situations, including a threat from an unexpected source: her cousin Mary, Queen of Scots.

Mary was an infant when her father died and left her the throne of Scotland. Mary left the country and was raised in France while a series of officials kept her place on the throne. She eventually returned to Scotland to claim what was hers in 1561 (less than three years after Elizabeth began reigning as Queen).

Elizabeth had already worked to remove the presence of the French from her neighboring country of Scotland, but Mary threatened to undo all of that work. She was very connected to the French, and was a devout Catholic. Once again, it seemed like the question of religion was about to tear a country apart and lead it to war. Mary did not support a treaty that Elizabeth had signed, and one scandal after another made it clear that Mary was bringing Scotland closer and closer to civil war.

Finally, the people of Scotland rose up and forced Mary to give her throne to her son James VI, while she was arrested and sent to live in a prison castle. When Mary escaped and went to Elizabeth for help, it's not hard to understand why Elizabeth had mixed feelings over how to react. Even though they did not agree on many important issues, Mary had gone through many of the same ordeals that Elizabeth had: she had never really known her parents; she had been forced to give up the throne that was rightfully hers; and she was made to live as a prisoner in a large castle.

Elizabeth wanted to help her family member and fellow monarch to get her throne back, and she might have done so if it weren't for the advice of William Cecil and the rest of her Privy Council. They helped Elizabeth to see that Mary, Queen of Scots, was a woman who simply did not stand for the same things that Elizabeth did. Mary put her personal ambitions ahead of others, and if she were made Queen of Scotland again she might end up causing trouble for England.

Faced with the terrible decision of what to do, 28 year old Elizabeth chose to put her cousin Mary into prison for nearly 19 years before finally having her executed as a traitor (there was firm evidence that, while in prison, she had plotted to have Elizabeth killed).

Even though there were some people who didn't agree with Elizabeth's efforts to unite all Englishmen together and not to support Mary, Queen of Scots, most of the citizens of England loved Queen Elizabeth. Unlike Henry, Edward, and Bloody Mary, Elizabeth really cared for the people around her, and folks could sense that she wanted to make their lives better. In fact, Elizabeth regularly took rides in her carriage through the countryside (she called these trips "progresses") so that she could see the towns and villages of her realm with her own eyes, and could find out what the people needed from their ruler.

As Queen, Elizabeth did not fight many wars, instead encouraging her people to do what they could to make England a better place. She attended plays of William Shakespeare and supported explorers like Francis Drake as he travelled to the New World and circumnavigated the Earth. English privateers (like Drake) helped England to fight an unofficial "war" against the Spanish by stealing gold from their treasure galleons as they left the New World and returned to Spain. In fact, Francis Drake would soon become one of the most important members of Elizabeth's military during the fight with the Spanish Armada.

Elizabeth had defended England from multiple enemies during her reign, including France and the Dutch. But Spain had become more and more aggressive during her reign and eventually decided to invade England in 1588. They wanted to stop the harassment of privateers in the New World and they wanted to take England's throne for themselves (something Spanish King Philip II failed to do when Elizabeth wouldn't marry him).

The Spanish fleet (called the "Armada") was the most powerful group of ships in the world, but Elizabeth was confident that her country could defend itself against this powerful enemy. King Philip planned to sail his fleet up the coast of

Europe before picking up more troops in Belgium. Then this huge army would cross the English Channel and march on London, hopefully convincing English Catholics to join him and help him easily win the day.

7

But Philip II didn't count on how tough the English Navy was or how hard it would be to get the troops from Belgium without a deep port to dock his ships.

Rallying her troops before the battle, Elizabeth said: "I know I have the body of a weak, feeble woman; but I have the heart and stomach of a king - and of a King of England too."[8] Her words united the men and they went off to fight full of confidence and love for their Queen.

The English had longer range guns and faster ships, but the Spanish were able to use a special crescent formation to defend themselves, so after two minor battles neither side had gained or lost any ships. Then the Spanish went and anchored their ships to pick up the promised solders, and that was their biggest mistake. The shallow waters made them perfect targets for the English fire boats – boats loaded with explosives, lit on fire, and pushed towards the enemy. The boats drifted towards the Spanish and caused the captains to panic and search for deep water.

Once they broke formation and moved into the English Channel, disaster struck the Spanish: strong winds forced them to go North through the English Channel and around the coasts of

[8] Quotation source: http://www.bbc.co.uk/history/people/elizabeth_I

Scotland and Ireland. In the process, some 50 Spanish ships were wrecked on the coasts, and only about half of the Spanish sailors making it back to Spain alive.

Thanks to the hard work of commanders like Francis Drake and the unexpected winds from Mother Nature, the Spanish threat was removed and England became the most powerful nation with the strongest navy in the world. All of this happened under the reign of Queen Elizabeth.

Queen Elizabeth was popular. Her nation was thriving and her people loved her. But could this perfect situation last forever?

Unfortunately, no.

Chapter 3: The Later Life of Queen Elizabeth I

Queen Elizabeth never married, which was quite unheard of at the time. Some historians think that the Queen's bad experience with Thomas Seymour as a teenager made her avoid any romantic relationships, while others think that her reason had more to do with her deep love for her country, and her desire to give all her time and energy to the people of England.

Until the day she died, people called her "The Virgin Queen". In fact, when English explorer Sir Henry Raleigh went to the New World, he named the land he settled "Virginia" in honor of Queen Elizabeth and her famous virginity.

But that's not to say that Elizabeth did not know how to use her singleness to her advantage; she was known to let single rulers of other nations think they might be able to marry her some day, and she would use their constant attention to get favors for her country.

Elizabeth had a special reason to focus on her country: her personal advisors John Dee and William Cecil had convinced Elizabeth that she was to have a special role in the history of England: she was to help England grow from being just a small European country to a true worldwide empire. Her actions could set the foundation for this growth, but she would have to make wise decisions while she was still alive.

With these big plans in mind, Elizabeth wanted to make sure that England got its foot in the New World. Spain was already conquering nations across the Atlantic and England wanted to do the same. So on March 25, 1584, she sent a group of people to the New World to set up an English colony in Roanoke, Virginia. Although the settlement didn't have the success anyone had hoped for, it was an important first step towards English presence in the New World. Shortly after her death, Jamestown would be the first permanent settlement in what is now the United States.

With her successful reforms at home and actions abroad, Elizabeth had gained a very good reputation for herself. Up until the attack of the Spanish Armada in 1588, things went well for Elizabeth. But shortly after that famous battle – during a time that some historians call the "second" reign of Elizabeth – the Virgin Queen saw her reputation change and the love of her people begin to cool off.

The economy of England suffered four bad harvests in a row, and began to have serious problems. Even though the Queen did her best to help her people and to make sure that they got the food they needed, her best efforts just weren't good enough. English men and women began to riot in the streets, complaining that food prices were too high, and in a flash the people forgot how hard their Queen had worked for them.

Historians say that one of the main reasons why the people began to turn on Elizabeth had to do with her Privy Council. By the second half of her reign, her best advisors had died and the new people that Elizabeth had chosen were not as noble as the first group. Instead of using their intelligence and wisdom to help the country, these high-ranking officials fought to get attention and favors from the Queen and began to persecute Catholics much as Bloody Mary had done. Perhaps as a result of all the corruption in the royal court, the people of Ireland rebelled against English rule.

A few decades earlier, Elizabeth had suffered a personal blow and got sick with smallpox. The disease left her scarred and partially bald, which means that for the rest of her life Elizabeth had to use wigs and lots of makeup to cover up the damage. But because Elizabeth was surrounded by people who wanted her favor, and they would tell her each day how beautiful she looked - even though it may no longer have been true. One of these constant flatterers was the Earl of Essex, and it seems that in later years Elizabeth actually started to believe some of the things he said about her.

One day, the Earl failed in his duties as a military commander, and then when punished, rebelled against the Queen. He was accused of saying that only members of the Spanish royal family had the right to sit on the throne of England. Because of his words and actions, the Queen was forced to sentence her friend and confidant to death, and the Earl was finally executed in 1601 at the Tower of London; he was the last person ever to be killed in that famous prison. Perhaps it was around this time that Elizabeth began to realize that her personal judgment was not as sharp as it used to be.

Towards the end of her reign, Elizabeth thought more and more of the legacy she would leave behind. Unlike her siblings Edward and Mary, she had enjoyed the privilege of ruling the country for many decades. But because she had never had any children, it was the changes and decisions that she made which would live on long after she had died. So in 1600, Elizabeth formed a new organization for the betterment of England: the East India Trading Company.

The main goal of the East India Company would be to give England a foothold in India and to get more money flowing into the country. The East India Company would deal in tea, opium, and other goods, and would eventually become so powerful that it would have its own army that could govern several colonies.

The East India Company would go on to play a very important role in world history, not only on the Indian subcontinent but also in the formation of the United States. Later – almost two hundred years after Elizabeth died – there was a terrible famine that swept across Bangladesh and killed one out of every three people there. The East India Company lost almost all of the money they had invested in that area and the situation got worse, when shortly after all of Europe went through severe economic problems and could no longer do business with the Company. In the early 1770s, there was a real chance that Elizabeth's creation – the East India Trading Company - could go bankrupt.

The representatives of the Company went to Parliament and begged King George III and the other politicians to do something to help them, and to help preserve the legacy of England's beloved Queen Elizabeth. Parliament responded in 1773 by passing the Tea Act, which said that American colonies could only buy tea from the East India Company – paying all the taxes that had been forced on them by Parliament.

The colonists, of course, refused to buy the tea and pay the taxes, saying that King George was taxing the colonists without representation and their permission – treating them more like slaves than valued citizens. Sick of being forced to support the East India Trading Company, on December 16, 1773 the colonists dumped many boxes of English tea into Boston Harbor during an event that came to be known as "the Boston Tea Party."

Although there was no way that she could have known it at the time, the very company that Queen Elizabeth helped to create would play a major role in American independence decades later.

By 1601, it was clear that the Queen was getting very tired or her life and duties. She had lost so many friends through the years, and she was no

[10] Image source: http://upload.wikimedia.org/wikipedia/commons/thumb/e/e6/Boston_Tea_Party_w.jpg/300px-Boston_Tea_Party_w.jpg

longer as beautiful and lively as she had been as a girl. She loved her country, but now it seemed as if her country didn't need her like it did before.

On November 13, 1601, Elizabeth appeared before Parliament to talk about some economic issues, but she took advantage of the occasion and gave a sort of farewell speech. In the speech, she made it clear that this would be her last appearance before Parliament, and in one particularly emotional moment she said:

> "There will never queen sit in my seat, with more zeal to my country, care for my subjects, and that sooner with willingness will venture her life for your good and safety, than myself... And though you have had, and may have many princes, more mighty and wise, sitting in this state; yet you never had, or shall have any that will be more careful and loving."[11]

Yes, even as she prepared for the end of her long reign, Elizabeth couldn't help but repeat the fact that no one would ever love the people of England as she had. It was love for England that had motivated all of her actions – from unifying

---

[11] Quotation source: http://www.emersonkent.com/speeches/golden_speech.htm

the peoples' religions to staying single and never having any children.

After giving her final speech before Parliament (which came to be known as the "Golden Speech"), Elizabeth hid herself away in her home, and the people of England did not see or hear much of their beloved Queen. Because of old age and disappointments in life, Elizabeth had lost her will to live and her body slowly gave up its fight to stay alive. On March 24, 1603, Queen Elizabeth I of England died.

She was 69 years old and had sat on the throne for more than 44 years. With her death, the Tudor dynasty of English royalty came to an end and the House of Stuart began its rule.

The nation was stunned at the sudden death of this woman who had lived to serve them. But soon they were celebrating the coronation of a new king – Elizabeth's nephew James VI of Scotland. This son of Mary, Queen of Scots, chose a new name once he became King (James I of England), and finally united the two countries together under one government.

Although he became briefly obsessed with hunting witches, overall, he continued the religious tolerance started by Elizabeth, and the nation flourished under his rule. He even supported a modern-language translation of the Bible (the King James Version) which is still used in English-speaking churches around the world today.

By the time she died in 1603, Elizabeth was viewed by some people as a silly old woman who shouldn't be in charge anymore. But a few decades after her death, when the House of

Stuart failed to live up to their expectations, many English citizens looked back on the reign of Elizabeth, and realized what a jewel they had in the Virgin Queen. She had been a wise, even-tempered, generous, and thoughtful ruler. Those who sat on the throne after her made many wish that Elizabeth were alive and ruling again.

Chapter 4: Why Queen Elizabeth I Was Important

Queen Elizabeth had a life that read like a novel. In some ways it could have been a happy fairy tale: she was born into a royal family, travelled across the country in a horse-drawn carriage, and won the battle against the Spanish Armada. But in many respects, her life was also like a tragic play: she was disowned by her father, there were conspiracies against her life, she lost the love of her countrymen, and she was disfigured by a terrible illness.

But through all of the twists and turns of her amazing tale, Elizabeth always found a way to use her good judgment and strong personality to come out on top. Even though she found herself in a lot of situations that she would have preferred to avoid, she never let the negative pressure around her crush her spirit or push her into making bad decisions.

The time period named after her – "Elizabethan England" – reflects how her personal struggles helped to shape the nation. The people of England learned to imitate their beloved Queen and not to let problems divide them and push them down. Under her rule, the arts flourished, and artists like Shakespeare gave us works that people still enjoy today while explorers like Francis Drake brought back tales of new parts of the world, and helped England to establish a presence on the other side of the Atlantic.

Queen Elizabeth lived her private life in the same way she lived her public life. As Queen, she said that it wasn't her job to judge others, and that she truly loved the people of England. She proved that in her private life by surrounding herself with many different types of people and by never looking for a husband or starting a family - instead choosing to be "married" to England.

This deep and personal commitment endeared Elizabeth to her people, and made them support even some of the more controversial decisions that she made. The support of the people for most of her reign also let Elizabeth leave a legacy as the founder of the British Empire, helping England to spread its influence to new parts of the planet, and to colonize one country after another. She helped the country to get one single national identity and culture and to be proud of who they were.

If Queen Elizabeth had never inherited the throne, England may have become a very different country. It may have continued to be plagued by religious differences, and many more citizens may have died. More wars may have been fought with France, and the Netherlands and England might have even been taken over by Philip II and the Spanish Armada. If that had happened, then the colonists sent out years later to the United States would have spoken Spanish, and Americans today would be speaking a completely different language!

If Elizabeth had never inherited the throne, artists like Shakespeare may not have received the support they needed to flourish, and explorers like Drake may never have gone to the New World. The East India Company might never have been founded, which would have changed the entire course of history on the Indian subcontinent and in the United States.

Elizabeth truly helped to establish the British Empire, and showed later rulers what a Queen should be and how she should act. Her example highlighted that a leader should be selfless and loving, and should make decisions based on what is good for the people, and not just what is good for the royal family.

Truly an example to imitate, Queen Elizabeth I of England will live on forever in the hearts of those who learn about her.

Made in United States
North Haven, CT
27 March 2023

34626642R00029